The Velveteen Killer Rabbit
Or How Toys Kill To Become Real

A Parody

by Elia Anie

Illustrated by
Elia Anie

www.VelveteenKillerRabbit.com

ISBN-13: 978-1480033115
ISBN-10: 1480033111

Other works by Elia Anie
Evil Penguins: When Cute Penguins Go Bad
Evil Cat: A Fluffy Kitty Gets Mean

List of Illustrations

The Mangy Donkey Tells His Story 13

The Nanny Solution 27

Elimination 33

Spring Time 37

Summer On The Grassy Knoll 43

The Substitute Fairy 53

Furry Fury! 63

To My Other Half

Even as I become shabbier (and bunchier),
he still loves me the same.

The
Velveteen Killer Rabbit
Or How Toys Kill To Become Real

Once there was a velveteen rabbit, who was fat and fluffy as a rabbit should be, and in the beginning he was magnificent.

His ears were lined with shiny pink satin, he had whiskers of fine thread, and his fur was pure white, except for a patch under his tail that was mysteriously spotted brown. But there was something not quite right about this bunny. It may have been the peculiar way his velveteen fur fell over his large, black eyes, or the slightly lopsided way his mouth was sewn, or it may have been a trick of the eerie lighting, but on Christmas morning, when he was stuffed into the Boy's stocking holding a dradle to look cuddly, the effect was oddly creepy.

In addition to the Rabbit and the dradle, there was a robot, a metallic train, a set of nativity scene action figures, a singing fish mounted on a plaque, a T-shirt depicting three wolves howling at a moon, and a fruitcake, all crammed into the stocking, but the Boy loved the fun packaging and the shiny wrapping paper with the ribbons the best. And when distant relatives from on far joyously gathered together on that festive day, and had merry conversations over a sumptuous feast, and while the grown-ups argued, fought, punched, and thrashed each other with the Velveteen Rabbit in a wine-sodden haze, the Boy amused himself with the empty boxes of various sizes and shapes and the crinkly sheets of colorful paper.

After the holidays were over, the Rabbit was all but forgotten, and idled his days away in the Boy's room, in his toy chest or closet, except when he was put to use as a door stop or a window jam.

Now and then, he found himself on the floor of the nursery, where he was trampled on repeatedly by the Nanny as she went wobbling about her daily tasks of cleaning and organizing. The Nanny, too, was fat and fluffy, but like a great many stuffed rabbits put together. She had a patch over her right eye due to a "manatee feeding incident" which removed her depth perception; as a result, she often stumbled about the nursery, walking into obstacles and tripping over things like an inebriated pirate wearing an inflated life jacket.

Being one of the new arrivals, the Rabbit was often teased by the other, fancier toys. The mechanical toys pretended that they were real, and buzzed and whirled about, and flashed their lights for a seizure-inducing effect. The jointed dolls boasted of their ability to move their limbs separately and rotate their heads all the way around, and looked down on those that couldn't. Even Tim, the teddy bear who was sewn by laid-off ten-year old sneaker-making children in China, pretended that he was connected with the mafia and was once used to smuggle "candy" into America from Colombia.

Soon, the new robot and train that had shared the stocking with him on Christmas morning joined them in talking tough, using most impressive words like "turbo-power", "velocity", and "unidirectional-hypercontinuum-phase-capacitance". The robot also proudly flaunted his big gun, and cautioned the others how dangerous it was for anyone standing too close. Every night, the Rabbit would see him polishing his mighty weapon with great care, satisfactorily firing off a round each time at the end.

But the most haughty of the bunch was a slender plastic doll with soft blonde hair. Thinking of herself as better than everyone else, she often raised her little plastic nose in disdain at the crass and unsophisticated playthings around her. She chattered endlessly about how beautiful she was to anyone that would listen, and bragged about how the Real women were having something called "procedures" done to look more like her, inserting or removing various objects, liquids, or hair as needed until the goal was achieved.

The Rabbit mostly listened as he had no moving parts, batteries, or flashing lights to boast of. Since he wasn't jointed either, when he tried to move his arm or leg, the rest of him would follow grudgingly, as though he were a damp, slightly-used sack of flour animated by a magician.

His shortcomings were not lost on the other toys. With contempt, the snobbish plastic doll with the overexaggerated lady-bits pointed out the Velveteen Rabbit's deficiencies at every turn, while the robot with the glistening, well-buffed rifle buzzed circles around him, laughing. Even the dust bunnies left behind by the myopic Nanny gathered gregariously in various corners of the room and taunted him for his shapelessness. Only the three-legged Donkey was kind to him.

The mangy Donkey had been around much longer than the others, and spoke often of the bygone days when Mammoth toys ruled the nursery. In fact, he was so old that his large ears were in tatters, his one eye dangled loosely by a coarse thread, and there were many patches where the brown fur had worn off as if he was locked in a closet with a dozen starving moths for a week. Here and there his nasty innards oozed out of the gaping holes where the seams had broken, and during one chilly season, a family of mice had nested cozily inside him, leaving behind little dark pellets which slowly rotted and gave off a foul odor.

As for the Donkey's missing leg, it could be said that it was "loved off" by his original

The Mangy Donkey tells his story

owner during a long series of encounters that one summer when it wouldn't stop raining. Further, his tail was a mere clump of grimy strands of filaments that he arranged proudly, like a plump old man clutching defiantly to the last wisps of his hair combed futilely over his bald pate.

Being old, the Donkey had lived to see all the fancy toys arrive flaunting their superior qualities, only to quickly break and be tossed away. Despite their arrogant boasts, he knew that they were just toys and would never be anything more. For the toy magic is strangely wondrous, and only the decrepit and wise playthings like the gimpy Donkey had been pounded over and over with it.

One day, the horizontally-endowed Nanny marched straight into the door frame of the nursery, causing the wooden timbers in the support structure to groan and creak in feeble protest. Partially protected by her considerable natural cushioning, she bounced off and stumbled onto the Rabbit, then kicked him spitefully into the toy closet. With the grace of a stuffed ostrich being catapulted into the air by a one-armed monkey, he fell lying next to the mangy Donkey.

"Tell me, what does it mean to be REAL? Is it having batteries and flashing lights and being the master of a magnificent gun?" the Rabbit asked the three-legged animal.

The lame equine shifted slightly so that his dangling eye could better see the Rabbit without making him dizzy. "It isn't what you're made of that makes you Real. It happens when a child loves you very much, not just as a toy, but really loves you. Only then do you become Real."

"Are you real?" asked the Rabbit, as he was very nosy and liked to pry into others' affairs.

"Yes, the Boy's stepmother's cousin's brother with the missing front teeth made me real. It was a long time ago, but once you become Real, it is forever," replied the Donkey.

The rabbit studied his friend's badly mangled features for some time.

"It looks like it was painful."

"When you're Real, you don't mind it," said the mangy Donkey. "And you don't care that you're grotesque, smelly, and just plain revolting to be around, so that people nearby want to gouge their eyes out with a plastic spork, because to those that matter and understand, you'll never be ugly. Although to be frank, I could have done without the requests to 'squeal like a pig' during the process."

The Rabbit saw how dreadfully hideous the Donkey was, and realized that the Boy's stepmother's uncle's nephew's brother with the missing front teeth must have really loved the Donkey like no other. He then understood why the haughty robots and cars that buzz and flash for a while and then break will never be loved by a child long enough to become Real, and this made him feel better.

Although at first the idea of looking as if he were run over by a rickety train carrying a herd of Nannies in both directions made the Velveteen Rabbit fearful, he wanted to know what it felt like to be Real, and this fancy occupied him day and night. He would have to be loved by a child first, but how could the Boy notice him if he didn't have glittering lights that flashed, jointed limbs, or a gun so massive that it would make others slack-jawed in awe?

While he was dreaming of becoming Real, the snobbish plastic doll continued to mock him, always eager to ridicule his cheap, polyester content. This made the little Rabbit so miserable that his velveteen fur began falling off onto the floor, which made more mess to be cleaned up, which made the Nanny spend more time in the nursery, which resulted in more trampling incidents for the Rabbit, which made him more miserable and made him shed even more fur.

One day, the doll was admiring herself in the mirror, too engrossed with her reflection to see the little Rabbit approaching her, dragging a rubber chicken that the Boy sometimes strangled to relieve stress.

Without warning, the Rabbit swung the semi-elastic fowl and struck her full across the face, knocking her off her dainty feet with such force that one of her legs came off. Picking up her detached limb, he whacked her again and again with it, until her little head popped off, flew across the room, plunged into the fish bowl with a little *plop*, then finally came to rest on the bottom, where the goldfish nipped voraciously at the fair hair that whipped about softly like a wispy sea plant. After that, the other playthings left him alone.

* * *

"Do you think the Boy will ever love me?" the Rabbit asked the three-legged Donkey one day.

He felt bad about being thrown at the ragged ass earlier. The Nanny had come in to the nursery and decided that she didn't like the way the Rabbit was throwing off the spatial balance of the room with where he was, so she had hurled him onto the tattered Donkey, where he became tangled on the exposed thread of his dangling eye for a long, awkward minute. On trying to free himself, the Rabbit tugged it an inch farther down before disengaging himself and falling to the floor clumsily.

"Selfish toys do not deserve to be loved. They are mean-spirited and care only about themselves. The universe has no place for such self-serving creatures," said the Donkey in his all-wise, patronizing way.

The Rabbit was at first becoming very drowsy watching the Donkey's pendulating eye, but when his friend's cruel words had finally registered, he was devastated. He felt his inside crumple up into a tight little ball. It was as if someone had ripped off his tail, then yanked his entire polyester stuffing out through his rear hole in one, powerful jerk. He became livid.

"What do you know about being Real? You're not Real. You just lied about it to make yourself look important like the others, bragging how wise you are and how the Boy's stepmother's cousin's nephew's uncle's – how the Boy's distant relative with the missing front teeth 'loved' you." The Rabbit recalled what the others had told him about the mangy Donkey. "REAL donkeys don't sit around in the nursery all day. They run outside on all four legs with the other donkeys."

Then he gave a sharp push on one of the equine's three remaining legs, making him tip over and hit the floor so hard that his optic nerve-like thread snapped and the dangling eye rolled to the middle of the room; there it lay all night, staring accusingly at everything around it in mute horror.

The next morning, they came and took the Donkey away.

After the Nanny finished supervising the grim task of removing the fallen ass, she noticed the little Rabbit slumped in the corner of the room, facing away. She thought it strange how she had always found him in odd places despite having put him away, like just a few days ago when she discovered him by the window with the headless doll's blonde hair all over him. She picked up the Rabbit suspiciously and said, "I declare if that old Bunny hasn't got quite a sinister expression!"

Then she threw him into the closet, but lacking depth perception due to her cyclopean condition, she missed the intended shelf and the Rabbit tumbled back out onto the floor. Shortly after, she tripped over him and hit her bulbous head on the dresser, narrowly missing her uncovered eye on the sharp corner of the furniture.

Seething with anger, she kicked the Velveteen Rabbit at the toy chest, but missed and smashed her foot hard on the wooden box and let out a loud cry. Crumpling into a massive and formless heap in agony, the Nanny convulsed with rage.

Her plump face turned so red that the little Rabbit thought he heard a bead of sweat sizzle on her greasy face. She picked up the Bunny and throttled him with such force as if to make him excrete a creme-filled chocolate egg. Not satisfied with the result, she threw him against the wall in disgust and left the room panting heavily – but only after slamming into the side of the door first.

As time went on, the little Rabbit was becoming more ragged and dingy from all the abuse he was receiving from the Nanny. Depending on how the fat woman stepped on his head, his eyes either became closer together, or further apart, neither of which made him look cuddly, he thought. With anguish, the Rabbit saw that he was slowly turning mangy like the three-legged Donkey – and the Boy hadn't even had a chance to love him yet. This would have to change, he decided.

Days later, when the Boy was out to a funeral for an old relative who was last seen at the Christmas gathering being clobbered on the head with a flaky dinner roll, the Nanny came stumbling into the nursery like a corpulent tumbleweed to "tidy up". She waddled around the room flinging and hurling things madly while muttering to herself.

Suddenly, in the middle of the room, she stopped. On the floor in front of her was a sharp tack with the pointy side up, as if patiently waiting. Staring at it with her mouth gaping open, she stood there for such a long time that drool gathered in the corner of her orifice. She finally picked it up carefully with her stubby fingers. With her eyes still on the pointy thing, she was turning toward the trash bin when her foot stepped on a toy car that seemed to appear from out of nowhere. The car rolled forward, and she fell back with a loud thud, sending all the toys in the nursery bouncing into the air for a brief second.

Before she had a chance to grasp what had happened, a fluffy little bunny crept out of the shadows, lurched toward the door and slammed it shut – with her head in the way. The Rabbit opened and closed it repeatedly on her round, globular head until her elephantine body slowly stopped undulating completely.

The little Rabbit was exhausted. There was blood splattered everywhere. With his ears lowered halfway in mourning, he observed a moment of silence for the fallen toy car that was crushed beyond recognition.

Just as he started lumbering away from the door, a broad leg came down in front of him and pinned him to another in a crushing lock. The Nanny was still alive – and not very happy. She squeezed her thick thighs firmly together in a masterful show of dexterity, as if she had wrestled stuffed toys many times before, and the little Rabbit began to slowly disappear into her fleshy folds.

Just then, he saw the tack on the floor nearby, its sharp, pointy end sparkling radiantly in a halo of light. With singular determination, he stretched for it with all his polyester might, grabbed it, and jabbed it into her bulky leg. She let out a horrible scream and momentarily released him from her vice-like grip.

The Rabbit clambered toward the sharp pair of scissors that the Boy kept on his desk, but before he could reach them, a grubby hand grasped him by his lower half and dragged him back, hoisted him up into the air, and smashed him against the blood-smeared door several times. Slowly, the pudgy fingers closed around the Rabbit's neck and tightened.

As he struggled feebly, the Nanny glared at him with her one good eye, pulling him closer and closer, her lonely bloodshot orb becoming larger and larger to the Rabbit until it filled his entire field of vision. With his velveteen paw, he made a decisive lunge, poking her in her evil eye, and she recoiled, howling in pain.

The Nanny thrashed about on the floor, hitting and grabbing at everything around her, and shouting things that were not very nice. Soon, the Boy's blanket and pillows came tumbling down to the floor, wrapping around the Nanny. The more she squirmed, the more entangled she became, so that her once destructive arms were rendered impotent by the bedding like an angry octopus in a straightjacket.

With her powerful limbs neutralized, the little Rabbit grabbed a fluffy pillow and threw himself valiantly onto the Nanny's greasy, blood-spattered face, covering the blowholes until she stopped moving. Not confident that

The Nanny solution

she wouldn't come back from the dead again like a villain from some crappy horror film, he sat a full minute longer with the saliva-soaked pillow in place. Then he lumbered to the toilet and washed himself clean of blood.

The next day, a new nanny was shown the nursery. She was much younger, lighter, and prettier, and seem to have a bit of spunk. Accidentally tucked in the back of her skirt at the waist was a little piece of toilet paper, which moved like a fluffy tail when she walked about the room. This immediately endeared her to him.

The Rabbit soon observed that this new yellow-haired nanny was not the brightest bulb on the Christmas tree, and at times, failed to light altogether. She became confused easily, and sometimes found herself locked in or out of the nursery. He would hear her pulling and tugging on the door handle from the outside when she should have been pushing, and once inside, she would be pushing and leaning on the door with all her little body when she should have been pulling on it.

From then on, he saw the pretty nanny every day.

* * *

Now that the Nanny issue was "resolved", the little Rabbit was able to pursue his dream of becoming Real. Remembering all that the three-legged Donkey had told him of the toy magic, he tried to find a way to be the most lovable of all the Boy's toys, even spending hours practicing various cuddly poses in front of a mirror, hoping he would someday be noticed.

With jealousy and envy he watched the Boy in bed with a red-headed doll. Every night, he would kiss "Ann" on her red nose and hold her tightly until he fell asleep. The little Rabbit imagined himself in bed with the Boy, having his pink, plastic nose kissed, and being held in his arms lovingly until he drifted off to sleep.

He even tried to hug himself to see what it would feel like, but his arms were too stubby, and no matter how hard he tried, he just couldn't get them to wrap around himself. This made him more depressed, and after several attempts, he gave up in frustration. Oh, how he wished to be hugged by the Boy! But he knew that this dream would never come true with Ann in the Boy's bed.

One night, when the Boy fell asleep, the little Rabbit wriggled out of the toy chest and crept close to the bed. In the moonlight, the doll's face looked so serene and radiant as she slumbered happily in the Boy's embrace.

He stared at this peaceful image for some time before dragging her out of the bed by her thick, red hair. With the doll whimpering helplessly, he dragged her across the nursery floor, then he dragged her to closet. He dragged her here, he dragged her there, he dragged her everywhere, until her hair started falling out yarn by yarn. He finally dragged her into the potty room, and the following morning, the pretty nanny discovered a very raggedy Ann with her head in the toilet.

When it was time to go to sleep, the Boy couldn't find his red-headed doll. He looked under the blanket, glanced under the bed, and even peeked under the lamp, but his Ann was nowhere to be found. The pretty nanny went about the nursery looking for a replacement, because she knew the doll wouldn't be found no matter how hard she was looked for. When she noticed the Rabbit primely positioned and looking as cute as he possibly could, she yanked him up by the ear and threw him onto the Boy's bed.

"Here's your Bunny. You can sleep with this one," she said.

From that point on, the Rabbit slept in the Boy's bed. At first, it was strange and irritating, like when the Boy drooled on him, or hugged him too tightly on the head, making his plastic eyes bulge out. Sometimes he snored so loudly that the Rabbit would lie awake all night in agony with his stuffing in a bunch, awaiting the coming dawn.

Then, it got even worse. The Boy would babble endlessly about the most mind-numbingly frivolous things so that at times, the Rabbit felt like wrapping his long ears around his fluffy bunny neck and pulling them tight until he passed out, thus being spared the Boy's inane gibberish.

On some nights the Boy would whimper loudly, and hold the Rabbit very close to him, so that his velveteen face and ears would become damp with the Boy's tears and runny nose snot. And at other times, while still seemingly asleep, the Boy would suddenly yell and pummel the Bunny with his little fists like he was fighting ninjas, then fall still again, murmuring something.

Now that the Velveteen Rabbit had the attention of the Boy that he had craved for so long, he simply found the creature

Elimination

insufferable. With unenthusiastic patience, he waited for the day when the Boy's love would make him Real.

As time went on, the daily hugs, kisses and sleep-beatings took their toll on the little Rabbit. Several patches on his soft velveteen fur were threadbare, and his dominant ear was beginning to rebel impudently and separate from the rest of him. He was also getting noticeably paunchier from being grabbed and hugged under the arms and head, which crammed the polyester stuffing inside down to his lower half.

And the once-luxurious fluff on his tail was almost gone to a wisp during an incident when the Boy's grape-flavored chewing gum had become stuck there and his backside had to be shaven. If the nanny hadn't stepped on the Rabbit and caused him to push a giant, purple bubble out of his butt, then the Bunny's proctological condition may have gone undetected a while longer, and the outcome may have been far more disastrous.

When spring came, the Boy had tea parties in the garden. With giddy enthusiasm, he would slip on his mother's prettiest dress and her daintiest shoes and put on the brightest make-up, and they would have tea near the flower beds. Afterward, the Boy might braid the Rabbit's satin ears, much to the Bunny's annoyance. Sometimes, when he was feeling a bit moody, they would play the funeral game, which involved the Boy burying the Rabbit under a pile of dirt while reciting something and playing with a long, beaded necklace.

Once, while the Rabbit was still buried in the ground, the Boy felt an unpleasant bout of diarrhea coming on and ran home in panic, abandoning the little Rabbit. Earlier in the day, he had eaten a piece of chocolate that had fallen to the ground where it lay on the germ-infested surface for four full seconds, which was a whole second longer than what the medical experts of the day deemed safe to consume.

When bedtime came and his Bunny wasn't there, the Boy threw a hissy-fit and refused to stop until they found him. So the pretty nanny trudged in the garden with a flashlight until she spotted a pink ear sticking out of the ground, yanked the Bunny out from the soil, and then beat him soundly with a stick to shake loose all the dirt.

"All this fuss over a toy. Here," she said as she threw the tattered Rabbit by his ear at the Boy.

"My Bunny! He's not a toy. He's REAL! Don't listen to her," said the Boy as he hugged him tightly.

Hearing this made the little Rabbit very happy. So the mangy Donkey's story about the toy magic had come true, and he was Real at last! He heard the Boy say so himself!

Spring time

He was so overcome with joy that it was difficult to sleep that night. The immense love for himself that filled his polyester heart transformed him so that, for a moment, the Boy's slimy drool on the Rabbit's grubby face glistening in the moonlight could have been mistaken for a radiant glow of wisdom and beauty.

* * *

What a gay summer it was! In the afternoons, the Boy liked to take the grumpy Rabbit to a grassy knoll nearby and have a picnic. Afterward, the Boy polished the nails on his fingers and toes with a bright shade of pink, and just before putting it away, dabbed a little drop of it on the Rabbit's plastic nose.

Now and then, if the Rabbit was lucky, the Boy would become distracted by a pretty flower in the distance, or the Rabbit would see him scurry past as he was pursued by a swarm of cantankerous butterflies, foul-tempered birds, or belligerent squirrels with beady eyes shrieking madly. Screaming and flailing his arms wildly, the Boy would disappear into the woods, get lost, and not return for a long while.

One afternoon, while the Rabbit was happily enjoying his solitude from the Boy, two strange creatures crept out from the tall bracken ferns nearby and moved slowly toward him. They were rabbits like him, only much fluffier and newer. There was something odd about the way they moved, making themselves fat and round one second and long and slender the next. It was as if an invisible Nanny was stepping on them this way and that, but he couldn't see anyone else around. Except for the soft sound of their padded feet and occasional rustling of leaves underneath, they moved silently, without buzzing or clicking, so that it was difficult to tell if they were battery operated or moved by wind-up mechanism.

For some time, they observed each other.

"You're a queer one," said the fluffy grey rabbit.

The Velveteen Rabbit just stared back mutely because he didn't know what to say. He would like to have played with them, have tea parties and play burial games, but he didn't want to show them that he had no batteries and gears to move his stubby limbs.

The other rabbit crept close to him and twitched his nose.

"You smell funny, too."

The polyester-stuffed Rabbit didn't know what that meant, except that it was related to the nose-twitching of the strangely morphing rabbits, but it didn't sound like a good thing.

"Can you hop like this?" said the rabbit with the grey coat as he hopped here and there, leaping over the grass.

The Velveteen Rabbit froze. He wasn't jointed, so he could only move by throwing his weight to one side and then to the other as his entire body lurched slowly forward, dragging his bare bottom along.

"I don't want to. I just want to sit," said the Rabbit timidly.

"You can't, can you?" they challenged him.

"I can!" said the little Rabbit. "I can jump higher than anything!" He meant when the transversely-abundant Nanny had kicked him out of spite, but he wasn't going to say so.

The two fluffy rabbits crept closer to him until they were on either side of him.

"Hah! Look here!" cried one rabbit as he peeked behind him, pointing, and the other rabbit hopped around quickly to have a look.

"You have no hind legs!" he said, and they both broke into a hearty laughter.

"I do! I HAVE hind legs. I'm just sitting on them."

The fluffy grey rabbit jumped up and knocked him over, then sat on his dingy face so that they both could have a good look at his bottom.

"Look at his stumpy legs. They're stuck to his butt! Hah!" he exclaimed, and they laughed so hard that they butted their furry heads together.

The Velveteen Rabbit struggled to free himself but they were too heavy. Besides, there was a pink sack of hairy hare balls spread ignominiously over his face, and he could scarcely breathe.

"You're not a rabbit. You're not Real. You're a freak!" said the grey rabbit as he hopped off the Velveteen Rabbit's face.

"I am Real! The Boy told me!"

But they didn't care. Laughing merrily, the feral rabbits hopped off into the bracken.

Soon the little Rabbit was all alone. For a long while, he lay still and watched the carcinogenic fern that the two wild rabbits disappeared into, hoping that they would hop back and talk with him some more.

Slowly, the sun sank down behind the trees until it became dark. Field mice scurried forth

Summer on the grassy knoll

and tugged excitedly at the wisps of polyester stuffing curiously poking out through the broken seams at his leg, looking for nesting material, but the strange rabbits did not return.

As time went on, the little Rabbit became more tattered and filthy, but that didn't matter to the Boy who loved him just the same. It didn't matter that all his whiskers had been loved off and that his pink satin ears had worn to a dull grey – or that his one eye was becoming loose so that it appeared as if he was looking at two different things at once. It didn't even matter that the polyester entrails were spilling out defiantly from the numerous new orifices on his threadbare body, so that not even the courageous little Dutch boy could possibly stop all the leaks, because to the Boy, he was beautiful. Now that the Rabbit was Real, he didn't give a rat's fanny about what others thought of him.

And then, one day, the Boy became ill.

It was difficult sleeping with the Boy because he clutched the Rabbit so tightly that he scorched him with his feverish body. Strange people bustled in and out of the nursery at all hours of the day and fussed over him.

After a few days, a doctor came with a little jar of worm-like creatures, and attached them to the Boy's body. Upon being satiated, the segmented invertebrates fell off, but to everyone's surprise, this did not make the Boy's illness go away. The doctor then had the ailing Boy breathe deeply into a paper bag, but the Boy didn't get any better. Desperately, the doctor stood behind the pale, emaciated Boy and exerted abdominal thrusts, but this only made the Boy cough up vile slush. Exhausted, the doctor finally left, shaking his head.

The following day, a tall man dressed in black came into the nursery with a wooden cross, had the Boy's hands and feet tied to the bed posts, and shouted scary things at him before sprinkling some water on him from a little glass vial. The terrifying man gave the Bunny such a fright that he stayed hidden underneath the blanket.

As there was nothing to do because the Boy was too ill to play, the Velveteen Rabbit idled away his time staring at various objects in the room and trying to move them telepathically. Not being successful because of his two eyes disagreeing on which object to look at, he soon became bored and restless.

While waiting for the Boy to recover, the Rabbit soon realized that he had come to miss those things that he found irritating at first. He missed the Boy's incessant chattering about trivial things, his damp and slimy kisses, and even the sleep-beatings at night.

Patiently, with tenderness and love, the Rabbit comforted the Boy and waited for that day when he would be well again. And all the wonderful things he had planned for them, all the little games they would play on the grassy knoll, and all the pretty dresses he would wear once he was well again, all this the little Rabbit whispered in the Boy's ear as he lay delirious in his sleep. Presently, the fever went away, and the Boy was able to sit up in bed and prattle nonstop about inconsequential things.

One morning, when they thought the Boy was well enough, they took him out for a little stroll in the garden. He was going to see a musical tomorrow, they said. Still in bed and hiding under the blanket, the Rabbit felt his little heart, which had been gradually pushed down toward his left leg, beat so fast with giddy elation that he thought it would burst. Finally, after countless weeks in bed, the Boy was healthy again, and tomorrow they were going to the theater together!

"Oh, the stench!" cried the pretty nanny with a grimace as she came into the room.

After throwing the windows wide open and catching some fresh outdoor air, she went about the task she had been given. Following the doctor's instruction, she began to take away everything the Boy had touched, coughed on, slobbered on, or urinated on.

Little by little, things around the Rabbit disappeared: the picture books made mushy with the Boy's drool, the grimy pillows, the sweat-soaked pajamas, the bedsheets, all into a sack the nanny was carrying. Suddenly, the blanket over him was snatched away and the little Rabbit lay horribly exposed on the bed.

"Gross!" cried the nanny as she shrank back from him in disgust.

Helplessly, she took a quick look around the room, grabbed the stick previously utilized to beat him clean, and used it to lift the germ-infested toy off the bed and drop him into the sack without touching the wretched thing.

The sack was then carried out and left behind a little shed by the edge of the garden, waiting to be burned in a bonfire that night. But the gardener entrusted with the task had other things he had to attend to first: some potatoes to hide under his bed, a few gardening tools to put away in his coat, and a bottle of whiskey to empty.

That night, while the Boy was asleep dreaming of tomorrow, the dingy little Rabbit lay on top of the rubbish, feeling very lonesome. The sack was left untied so he tried wriggling himself free, and just as his head popped out of the bag, a bird flew over and discharged its fecal slop on his head. He tried to wipe the wet mess away so that he could see, and this tipped him out of the sack he was in onto a giant cobweb. Without delay, the resident spider went to work tugging triumphantly at the Rabbit, trying in vain to drag him to its favorite dining space; having no luck, it gave up after much effort and retreated back to its hiding place sullenly.

Liberated from the sack and freed from the spider's spindly clutch, the little Rabbit started to shiver almost immediately, as he was used to sleeping in the cozy nursery, and his now shabby and threadbare coat was unable to keep him warm. Not even the delicate, silken web of dead flies and withered leaves wrapped around him provided much warmth.

In the bright light of the moon, the little Rabbit could see the garden where they had delightful tea parties together. He remembered those lovely sunny afternoons playing in the shade, and he became very sad. One by one, all that he had cherished flashed before him: the mani-pedi's on the grassy knoll, the lazy summer days being buried in the woods, and the Boy's histrionic reenactments of the bedtime stories. With a pang of sorrow, he recalled the immense joy he felt on first hearing the Boy tell him that he was Real – oh, how happy he was!

"What good was it to be loved and grow shabby and become Real if it all ends this way?" he lamented.

Then a single tear, a real tear, rolled down his ratty, poop-splattered cheek and fell to the ground. The little Rabbit was overcome with inconsolable grief and threw himself to the ground, pounding his little stumpy fists into the earth and raging at life's cruelty and the absurdity of it all.

The grief must have been overwhelming because he felt it dig into him – REALLY dig into him, boring into his innermost being like a knife of utter despair. Suddenly, he saw the world beneath him whirl away and he quickly became dizzy with misery.

What he didn't know was that at the very spot where the first Real teardrop fell, a seed had taken root, a seed of a magical flower, and after struggling to emerge from the ground under the Rabbit's belly, this strange and annoyed flower had thrust him high up into the air. Upon throwing out a few green leaves gratuitously, the bizarre plant blossomed impatiently into a most magnificent flower, like none the Rabbit had seen before.

When the flower opened her delicate, rumpled petals to reveal a lovely fairy inside glaring angrily, the little Rabbit was shoved to the side rudely and left to hang precariously onto the oversized yellow leaf for a long minute before falling back to the ground and landing on his tattered head. The little Rabbit was so battered and dazed that he quite forgot the reason for his grief.

"I suppose you're the little rabbit that's been bawling just now," said the Fairy irritably as she shook off some of the Rabbit's belly fur from her hair.

The Rabbit was a little embarrassed and stared at his grubby feet shyly.

The substitute fairy

"I'm the Tooth Fairy. I'm filling in for the Toy Magic Fairy, who is out sick because she's "allergic" to her fairy flower. She's probably sitting at home, eating ice cream and watching soap operas while claiming worker's comp. That lazy sea cow!"

She continued irately, "So now, I have to go around to all the old and shabby toys that the children had loved and no longer need and make them Real, and blah blah blah, and because of your stupid teardrop, I have to make you Real."

"But I thought I was Real," said the little Rabbit.

"Don't they all," said the Fairy, rolling her eyes. "You were real only to the Boy because he loved you, though the Boy ain't right in the head, if you ask me – he made a microfiber "security" blanket "Real" before you came along. But now that he no longer has use for you, I'll have to make you Real so that you're Real to everyone," said the Fairy. "But, you've been a bad rabbit. You have been very selfish and wicked. I'll show you what we do with rotten little bunnies."

And with that, the Fairy grabbed the Rabbit by the ear and flew with him into the forest.

It was a splendid night. The moon shone brightly in the sky, illuminating the magnificent trees and casting their dark shadows across the soft grass. High over the splendid nocturnal wonders they glided, and all the while the Fairy complained bitterly about her miserable job as the Tooth Fairy, and of the despicable children with revolting oral hygiene she was forced to barter with – especially the children in Britain. Below them appeared furry rabbits, hopping and dancing merrily with their shadows and bumping furry uglies, as rabbits are prone to do. As the Fairy and Rabbit descended, they all stopped prancing and mating and gathered around her.

"I've brought you a new playmate," the Fairy told them. "Try not to be too cruel, because you'll be stuck with him forever."

Then with the magic stick, she bonked the little Rabbit on his head so hard that a real tear squeezed out of his dingy face and fell to the ground once more, but no magical flower sprung out of the soil and attacked him this time.

"Now off you go, you little bugger," said the Tooth Fairy as she prodded him away harshly with the stick.

Rubbing his sore bum where she poked him, the Rabbit watched her fly off and disappear into the night, and hoped that he'd never have to run into the unpleasant fairy again. Then his mind went blank, for he saw that he was surrounded by fluffy rabbits, and they were all staring at him. He remembered the earlier encounter with the wild rabbits and thought that it would be best not to move; he didn't want to show that he had no hind legs and have a pudgy rabbit roasting his rump on his face again. What he didn't know was that the magical whack from the Fairy's stick had transformed him into a Real rabbit. But enlightening themselves of the true state of his backside no longer seemed to interest the feral rabbits. They continued watching him in silence, scrunching up their faces horribly like the pretty nanny did when she found something hideously repugnant.

"Which beauty product were they testing on you before they let you out?" one of them finally asked. It was the same rabbit with the grey fur that had personally introduced his bunny berries to him before.

Not understanding what he meant, the Rabbit just stared dumbly.

"Don't get too close or he'll eat your brain," growled a rabbit with a missing paw, while lumbering in place with the arms out in front of him, and they all broke out into a jolly laughter. Despite having his hand hacked off and sold as a lucky charm, he appeared to be in good spirits.

The mangy Rabbit found them all to be in a peculiar sense of humor, and without knowing he lifted his hind foot to scratch his head in bafflement – his hind leg! He had Real hind legs! A great rush of giddiness came over him and he glanced down at his lower half, and found that they were Real indeed – and dreadfully gnarly. Instead of a shiny, fluffy coat like the other rabbits had, his legs were covered with grimy, blotchy fur, as if he passed out in a goat pen and woke up a few days later. Horrified, the little Rabbit looked himself over and found that the rest of him was also in a repulsive state of nastiness. It appeared as though putrefying slabs of flesh were thrown carelessly over a bony structure. Additionally, in the middle of his belly was a putrid sore where the magic flower had tried to bore through, and a territorial maggot had already laid first claim to it.

In utter despair, he rushed to a nearby stream to check his reflection, but not being used to the new limbs he hopped and bounced wildly all over the grass and flew into a tree while the other rabbits roared with laughter. When he finally reached the water, the little Rabbit peered into the glassy surface and saw a grotesque creature, paunchy and badly mangled, as if he had fallen into a river infested with piranhas, then been carried out to the ocean and swallowed up by a sperm whale, then remained in its stomach for a full fortnight before being regurgitated out again. His head sank heavily into his formless torso. The Tooth Fairy had made him Real, but kept his old, decrepit body.

"Once you become Real, it is forever," the three-legged Donkey's words brayed loudly in his mind.

The little Rabbit wanted very much to weep again, but not a single tear appeared on his ratty, muck-caked face. He tried bunching up his insides in a desperate effort to squeeze out a tear, but instead little brown balls fell out from under his butt. He stared curiously at the mysterious cluster of round pellets that had just been expelled unceremoniously from his body; they appeared to be his Real insides spilling out of him – he was *dying*! The little Rabbit was devastated. What was the point of being loved and becoming Real, if it all ended with him dying this way? His monstrous little body began to shake with infinite anguish which, not being at all a pleasing sight to behold, sent the moon hiding for cover behind several smudgy clouds.

In a sudden fit of rage, he struck at the nearest rabbit first, kicking him with such ferocity that it sent the furry creature flying into the air and impaling him on a sharp tree branch. The skewered rabbit kicked and kicked trying to free himself until he couldn't kick any more, and then hung limply. The branch then snapped from the weight, sending the perforated rodent down through a prickly shrub to the ground. Shortly after, a coyote crept out of the shadows and dragged him away into the darkness again.

While the other rabbits watched in shock, the rogue bunny, formerly known as the Velveteen Rabbit, leaped at the grey rabbit and sank his nasty, big, pointy teeth into the fluffy neck and chewed cleanly through. Not since the valiant quest for the Holy Grail had a long-eared rodent so viciously attacked another living creature.

As the other rabbits all scrambled away and disappeared into the forest, the three-footed bunny nearby was too petrified to run, so he camouflaged himself as a bracken, hoping that under the pale, dim moonlight, he would blend right in. Standing on one foot, the cunning rabbit extended his other limbs and ears out like the fronds of a fern, and with his breath held anxiously, watched the rampaging Rabbit run past him without stopping.

Giggling in light of his good fortune, the crafty rabbit started to scramble in the opposite direction, but his good paw promptly became ensnared in a rusty trap. Unfortunately for him, the townspeople from the nearby village were none too pleased with the increasing feral rabbit population, which ate up their gardens and flowers; they had laid traps all over the forest to control the excessive rodent numbers. There, the rabbit with the missing lucky paw spent his final hours, reflecting on his misfortunes.

After the night of bunny butchery, the little Rabbit was sitting by a tree feeling quite miserable, when a crabby, arthritic squirrel, irritated at his hideous wretchedness, threw an acorn at him. In addition to leaving behind a sore lump on his misshapen head, the impact of the little nut knocked some sense into him, so that in the very brief moment of enlightenment that followed, the three-legged

Furry Fury!

Donkey's words of wisdom came hobbling back to guide him once more.

"To those that matter and understand, I'll never be ugly. The Boy will love me just the same," he declared, and a warm fuzziness spread over him, distorting his deformed mouth into a smile that was more grotesque than lovely.

His tender but fickle love for the Boy came flooding to him so that even his dark and murky eyes shone momentarily with inner grace and beauty before returning to their normal, scum-smeared, muddy state.

With the lovely image of the heartfelt reunion in mind, he slipped into the Boy's house and tiptoed quietly into the nursery, while the Boy was out to see the doctor. To his consternation, he found another rabbit on the Boy's bed. A furry new bunny, with brown spots all over its plush velveteen coat, lay snugly in HIS place. He decided this simply would not do. The brown-spotted bunny, with all its pristine newness, was dragged outside and thrown into a pit of dirt, then covered with more dirt until nothing, not even its pink satin ear, was visible.

After he was finished burying his fluffy doppelgänger, the decrepit Rabbit crept back into the Boy's house and lay in bed waiting. How good it felt to be back! While he waited, he thought about the delightful tea parties they would have again by the flower bed, and his heart was overwhelmed with dizzying excitement. Just then, he heard someone come into the nursery, and he immediately struck one of the cuddly poses he had rehearsed in the woods which he thought most suitable for the melodramatic occasion.

"Ahhhhhh!" the pretty nanny shrieked upon seeing a horribly disfigured, giant, mutant rodent sitting on the Boy's bed.

She pulled out a broom from the closet and began to beat the wretched devil over the head with it, sending the seemingly hell-spawned vermin crawling for cover underneath the blanket.

"Ahhhhh!" she continued, as she reached for the baseball bat leaning against the wall in the corner, and bashed the vile critter with it. The mass of putrefying rot from a demon's toenail that was the Bunny crawled out from underneath the blanket, wobbling dizzily, and this distressed her even more.

"Ahhhhh!" she shrieked again, as she backed away until she came to a wall and began hurling whatever she could get her hands on at the miserable inbred goblin, including a baby Jesus action figure, a singing fish mounted on a plaque, a very surprised and wet goldfish, and a rock-hard, stale fruitcake from the prior Christmas. The badly battered Bunny scurried down and crawled under the bed, but in no time, the broom found the infernal beast and was soon pommeling it on the head and body. The repugnant Rabbit scrambled out from under the bed and into the hallway, where the nanny, having run out of things to pelt it with, took off her shoe and hurled it at the ogre's congealing snot. She clomped after him noisily, like a peg-legged pirate with several pints of rum and a small bladder.

The wretched and battered critter found an open kitchen window and flung itself desperately through it, and disappeared limping badly into the bushes.

* * *

The next spring, the Boy was having a tea party on the grassy knoll with his red-headed doll – which looked remarkably like Ann, except that this one was wearing a sailor outfit – when he noticed a ragged, paunchy rabbit watching him from behind a tree. Having been discovered, the freakish rabbit scurried away, flipping his tail as he did so and showing faint brown spots on his hairless backside.

If the Boy had shown as much attention to the rodent as he did to braiding the doll's red hair, he may have found something oddly familiar about the rabbit's blotchy, shabby fur, and his smudgy, black eyes set eerily on his mangled face, and exclaimed:

"My Bunny! He looks just like the Bunny I had!"

But he never realized that the creepy rabbit that was stalking him was indeed his old Bunny, come back to look at the child for whom he had killed to be Real.

ABOUT THE AUTHOR

Elia Anie is an American author who lives with many stuffed animals in her cluttered den, including a fat and bunchy Rabbit. After a failed attempt by her Bunny to abduct her on her wedding day, Elia has been very watchful of the crafty stuffed rodent. At the time of publication, she has recently been reunited with her Rabbit after a period of separation – during part of which the stuffed Bunny was briefly placed in quarantine. (*This is really true!*)
The author vehemently denies that the Rabbit was ever threatened with winding up in a giant bonfire.

She is also the author of *Evil Penguins: When Cute Penguins Go Bad,* and *Evil Cat: A Fluffy Kitty Gets Mean.*